An
Account

of some of the most

Romantic Parts

of

North Wales

by

Joseph Cradock

—Of Antres vast, and Desarts idle,
Rough Quarries, Rocks, and Hills, whose Heads touch Heav'n
It was my Hint to Speak.

SHAKESPEARE

London
Hounskull Publishing
2023

HOUNSKULL PUBLISHING
BM Box Hounskull
London WC1N 3XX

An Account of Some of the Most Romantic Parts of North Wales
Originally published in 1777.

First Hounskull edition published 2023
© Hounskull Publishing 2023

ISBN 978-1-910893-23-4

TO

Sir WATKIN WILLIAMS WYNNE,

Bart.

SIR,

Every one will see the propriety of dedicating an Account of North Wales to You, who possess so considerable a part of that Country, and yet, Sir, this is not the motive of my Address;—it is from a high regard to that public and private Character which has hitherto been an ornament to Society, and which I trust will continue to adorn the Age with those Virtues,

of which your Ancestors were such eminent
Examples.

I have the Honour to be,
  with great respect,
    Sir, your obedient servant,
    JOSEPH CRADOCK.

Table of Contents

Note on This Edition
ix

Arms of the Principality
xi

An Account of Some of the Most
Romantic Parts of North Wales
1

Index
x

Note on This Edition

he text herein is based on the 1777 edition printed in London for T. Davies. It is herein reproduced in its entirety.

The punctuation, spelling, italicisation, and capitalisation has been left as in the original, except book titles referenced in the text have been set in Italics. Extensive quotations have been set as block quotes and taken out of quotation marks.

A complement of editorial footnotes has been added and identified as such.

In the index generated for this edition, the names of people and geographical locations appear in their conventionally accepted modern spelling; they are easy enough to match up with their counterparts in the original text.

ARMS

OF THE

PRINCIPALITY

BRUTE *gaue to* CAMBER *his Third Sonne,* CAMBRIA *with theise Armes, Tres Leones-Gradientesfacies mas   adterga vertentes in Campo Argentes,* In Frenche, Il portoit & Argent trois Lyons passants regardantes de Geules, *The which Armes the Kinges and Prynces of Wales and theire ofspringe, used fora Songe tyme after, untill the Country was deuided into three distant Pryncypa-lytyes viz:* North Wales South Wales and Powes Lande, *And then they tooke severall Armes.*

North Wales.

South Wales.

Powes Land.

An
Account
of Some of the Most
Romantic Parts
of
North Wales

s every one now who has either traversed a steep mountain, or crossed a small channel, must write his Tour, it would be almost unpardonable in Me to be totally silent, who have visited the most uninhabited regions of North Wales—who have seen lakes, rivers, seas, rocks, and precipices, at unmeasurable distances, and who from observation and experience can inform the world, that high hills are very difficult of access, and the tops of them generally very cold.

1

But ancient Britain has a kind of hereditary claim upon me, as I have the honour to
boast of my origin from thence; and as the
name and exploits of my ancestors continually occur through the wild heroic pages of
Welsh fable or history.

This journey was undertaken rather late
in the autumn 1776; the season proved remarkably favourable, neither rains, nor
winds impeded my progress—the air on
the mountains was left rarified by the sum-
mer's heat, the sun shone out all the day on
Cader, and Snowdon had not begun to for-
tify himself against this almost winter approach.

I set out from Shrewsbury for Welsh
Poole, the last eight miles afforded a most
beautiful prospect of a rich vale in Montgomeryshire. The Vales through out this
county are remarkably pleasant; but they
have been so frequently described, that it
is almost superfluous to observe, that they
abound with corn, and are luxuriant in pas-
turage.

Welsh Poole is a place of some note—it is
one of the five Boroughs in Montgomeryshire, which jointly send a member to Par-

liament. It has a good market, but though the Severn is navigable within two miles of it, there is scarce ever any fish—even salmon is never under twelve pence a pound. It takes its name from a contemptible black pool, which is said to be unfathomable, and of which there is a prophecy, that it shall some time or other overflow and deluge the town. This prophecy is still believed in Wales.

About a mile from hence stands Powis castle, or *Red* castle, from the colour of the stones of which it is built. The situation of it is certainly very noble, but I cannot agree with Lord Lyttelton, that three thousand pounds would make it the most august place in the kingdom; there is much to be done in the mere approach, and at present you are obliged to ask where the Severn runs. The ground is laid our in that formal style of gardening, that was brought in at the Revolution, and there will be much difficulty in altering it with propriety. A common Under taker in Taste, would immediately convert the clipt hedges and true love knots, into a gaudy and unmeaning shrubbery, but to decorate this place to advantage, the Genius of this place only must be consulted, "the parts[1] should every where be connected with each other, and must likewise bear a reference to the whole." On my return to Poole, I ordered a carriage to convey me to Llanvair this was to be my last stage on known ground, the road was perfectly good, the people in general spoke English, and their civility was so remarkable, that the very turnpike man was grateful for the toll. I was here most strongly recommended to a good house, about twelve miles distant, but found it only a miserable hut; I therefore pressed onwards as fast as possible, and after some difficulties arrived at Dynys Mouthy.

This City (for Dynys is Welsh for City) is possessed of many and great advantages; there is no body-corporate to divide it into faction, there is not a single Office that can possibly be contended for the rent of houses will be the same at all seasons, and even in August you are never incommoded by the sun. The river is not large, but it will never be encroached upon by the inhabit-

---

1   Pope.

ants; their sequestered walks will never be injured by any fresh Dealers in Taste, has deed they have only one tree to cut down, an oak planted in the reign of Charles the Second; and I believe they have never heard of any King since.

As to Fashions, they are similar to those in Town—the head dress of the Females is very high, and in a morning they generally wear the Half Polonese.[2]

The Inns too, like the London ones, are dark and dirty; but there is very little noise in them; and as to provisions, the people do not attempt to make what nature has not bestowed upon them. They gave the what-ever they had, Bread, uncontaminated with spurious mixtures, and Milk, that was absolutely from the cow.

I did not see a Cathedral, nor heard of either bishop or palace; probably he might reside at a great distance, and have consigned his flock over to a chapel of ease.

There is no court of judicature open here. This city is as free from attornies as ancient Thebes; indeed the two never failing dourc-

---

2   Jackets and petticoats.

es of litigation, the Poor laws and the Game laws, are entirely unknown. There is not even a Quack; so that those whom liquor spares, generally die at a very advanced age.

The Theatre is held in great repute. I had the pleasure to be present at one play, which is here called an *Anterlute*, probably a corruption from our term Interlude. The piece was said to have been written by a celebrated Mr. Evan something, who lived at Bala; but, from the *actions*, *gestures*, and *emblems*, I conceived it to have been modelled from before Shakespeare's time. The plot was in part similar to a burletta, which has frequently been exhibited in London, called *La Serva Padrona*, but the music was certainly *not* Pergolen. The orchestra, to be sure, was exceedingly contracted, but we must reflect, that some of our best, as well as earliest dramas, were only accompanied by a Harp. The price of admittance to this elegant entertainment would have been termed by the Romans, Denarius.

The road from Dynys Mouthy afforded but little amusement, and the first cast of Cader Idris greatly disappointed me; but I soon recollected, that as I was then on very high ground, it must have been from some other point of view that this mountain had rendered itself so remarkable. In the course of this reflection, I was on a sudden delighted with the country round Dolgelly,—woods, rocks, a rich vale, a fine river, and, at that distance, the appearance of rather a decent town, surrounded with many gentlemen's seats,—these, contrasted with the barrenness I had just travelled through, all joined to render the prospect truly delicious. But how was I disgusted on my arrival at the interior parts of this miserable place! there is no street in it; you pass from dungeon to dungeon, through a multiplicity of hog yards;—before I reached the inn I heard a cracked trumpet sounding every where about, and immediately concluded that I might see, in the evening, another farce or *anterlute*; but was informed it was only intended to call the Justices to the quarter-sessions. At the inn there was nothing to be obtained; so that as soon as possible I sent out for a Guide, that I might retire to the mountains; whilst I was in waiting, I enquired about the only tolerable building I then saw, and was told it was for cock-matches, such as we had in England;—that they were just over, but that I might go immediately and see a famous man from London shew *tricks of slight of band.* I chiefly wished for some refreshment, having greatly suffered from fatigue and illness the preceding day; but as I was a stranger, the people shewed me little or no civility, and on my enquiring for horses, took every advantage of my distress. I was now almost inclined to have bestowed upon them some rather ungracious epithets; but I considered, that as we seemed to be teaching them no thing from England but *cruelty* and *fraud,* I ought rather to lament the cause than insult the effect of their brutality.

On the arrival of the Guide, I set out immediately for Cader Idris, and found the tract exceedingly good, till I came to a prominent part of the mountain, and here, I must acknowledge, my head was too giddy sufficiently to admire the amazing scene that was opening to my view. At length, having gained the summit, (the whole ascent being near three miles,) on a fine piece of level ground, I could with comfort survey the sea, the Carnarvonshire shore, Snowdon without a cloud upon his top; lakes, rivers, rocks, and precipices which were every way spread before me;—at the bottom of the hill, on the opposite side, was a small Village, to which several were returning heavy loaden from Dolgelly market; this Village is remarkable for nothing but the remains of a small castle, whose miserable situation could not secure it from the depredations of Cromwell's army. In the course of my survey of the Mountain, it seemed to take a thousand capricious forms, but the most wonderful part of it is the tremendous peak, which over hangs the Lake of the Three Grains,[3] but here I shall for bear description, as a fine representation of it, has been lately executed, by the ingenious and accurate pencil of Mr. Wilson. On my return I discovered, far out of any tract, on the steepest part of the hill, a man gathering rockmoss to dye baizes red,—"dreadful trade!" one could only exclaim;—this excrescence is chiefly sold to Dublin—it affords a most beautiful colour at first, and if mixed with

---

3   The common people believe these three large craggs to have been cast out of the shoes of the giant Idris .

proper ingredients and distilled, will, it is said, become permanent. Being very thirsty from heat and fatigue, I enquired for some goat's milk, but to no purpose; the Guide, however, informed me, that he could procure me, from a neighbouring cottage, a liquor, peculiar to that part of North Wales, which infinitely exceeded Stirom cyder—I tasted it, and found it was made of mountain-ash berries and crabs or floes,[4]—it should remain at least half a year in the vessel be fore it is bottled off, and if it were then kept to a proper age, it would not be altogether contemptible. The tediousness of my return to Dolgelly, was somewhat beguiled by the consequential information of the Guide, and I must own he greatly entertained, and at the same time shocked me with the respect he paid me as an English gentleman,—whenever he replied to Me, he thought it necessary to interlard his answer with frequent oaths, whereas I found when

---

4   The following lines have since occurred to me:
         "Then she describes The Scythian winter, nor disdains to sing Howunder ground the rude Riphæan race Mimic brisk cyder with the brake's product wild; Sloes pounded, hips, and servis' harshest juice."

PHILIPS.

he spoke to my servant only, it was entirely in an unadorned style, without the least
display of these sensible embellishments.

The next morning being Sunday, I went
to eight o'clock prayers here—the area of
the church is spacious, and the pews neat,—
there is a coving roof of wood, which is necessary to aid the voice, as the floor is only
clay covered deep with rushes; the congre-
gation was large, and the service was read
with devotion and tolerable propriety.

My stay was prolonged at Dolgelly, that
the master of the Inn, who was absent on
my first arrival, and who was justly recommended to me as an intelligent Person,
might attend me to see the three wonderful waterfalls in this neighbourhood—one
of them is in so obscure a place, that the
minister of an adjoining Parish, whom I after wards met with, had never till that time
even heard of it:—about five miles on the
road towards Tan y Bwlch, we turned on the
left hand to see the first, which I take to be a
part of the river Dery—this is not more than
fifty feet in height, but you may afterwards
trace it, for near a mile, through crags and
trees, before it reaches its rocky bed at the

bottom; the others, are falls of whole rivers, the Mothwaye and the Cayne, over the tops of two rocky mountains;—the former perhaps may not be above one hundred feet in height, but the latter is certainly at least an hundred yards—both of them are shaded with beautiful woods on the sides of hills, whose summits are in the clouds, and whose feet are whitened by the foam of these tremendous cataracts.

Before we reached Tan y Bwlch, we stopped to look into a small church, where some cleanly villagers were assembled at evening prayers,—the women were by far the handsomest of any I saw in this country; the clergyman was reading the lesson concerning David and his Concubines, and I could not help reflecting, that if these ignorant people should any way confound the Old with the New Law, they might here find some excuse for that Gallantry, which sacrifices the virtue of so many females in this neighbourhood: to prevent such a mistake, would it not be proper to have an exposition made of this chapter, and translated into Welsh,—I mean only, provided the learned labour could be confined within the narrow limits of five volumes in folio.

I was much struck with the situation of Mrs. Griffith's house at Tan y Bwlch,—at first fight it somewhat resembled Matlock Bath, but the hills in front are thrown to a fine distance, and behind the house they are covered with wood;—through a very spacious valley the river Dryryd runs, and from the tops of the mountains are frequent and not inconsiderable cataracts,—indeed most of the romantic prospects of North Wales, taken separately, are infinitely superior to those of Derbyshire; but where shall we find within the fame distance, such amazing contrast as the high polish of Kedleston, opposed to the bleak horrors of the Peak.

Mrs. Griffith is possessed of a considerable fortune,—she has an only daughter, to whom a sensible clergyman, who resides in the house, is tutor, and who, though a chaplain, is treated as independent. A lady, it is true, in such a country cannot be every day interrupted with visitants, but Mrs. Griffith has generally a select party of friends, these form a rational society, whereas in many places, a good neighbourhood means little more than keeping an inn at your own expence.

At the distance of about three miles (the road most beautifully diversified) the scene changes on a sudden to some dark and naked precipices; at the bottom is a large rocky bason, which receives the Rhaidr-du, or Black Cataract, as it is called, —this, I am confident, is exactly similar to the spot where Hecate appointed her sister-witches to assemble, and offer their choicest incantations to complete the ruin of Macbeth.

> And at the pit of Acheron
> Meet me i'th' morning; thither He
> Shall come, to know his destiny.

The mistress of the little inn at Tan y Bwlch, has lived many years servant in considerable families, and from her attentive civility, has received great commendations from the few Englishmen that have hitherto visited this country.—Her house is this year much improved;—Lord Radnor, having staid a day or two there, has made her a present of the fitting up of her parlour: two sash-windows add great chearfulness to the room, and each grateful passenger readily joins with the landlady in celebrating the kindness of the public-spirited young nobleman.

The road to Harlech afforded great variety; there could scarce be more within the compass of ten miles. For the first three we the surveyed "the Happy Valley,"[5] we then passed by a beautiful lake, and having gained the next mountain saw the Castle, situated on a high rock, which projects into the Irish sea. It must be confessed, however, that the last two miles were rather "a staircase path;" but I have frequently travelled for twenty miles together in the midland counties of England with more danger and difficulty. In Wales one has the pleasure of seeing that they are making daily improvements in roads; but in England the farmers are so rich, that, by the aid of some petty attorney in the neighbourhood, they can generally protect perverseness by knavery.

Harlech stands on the north west side of the county of Merioneth; its houses are mean, and its inhabitants uncivilized. There

---

5   Vide Johnson's *Raffelas*.

is a good harbour for ships, but no ships for the harbour. It is remarkable only for its old decayed castle, which was defended by a British nobleman against Edward the fourth, till an earl of Pembroke, after almost incredible difficulties, compelled it to surrender. It has been confidently asserted that this castle was built before Edward the first's time, and that all he did was the making some additions, especially to the fortifications; but I should be rather inclined to think that it was planned at least by Edward. A tradition goes, that the workmen, after they had got to a considerable height, were all taken off to build the castles of Aberystwith and Carnarvon; and indeed there are evident marks of a Separation.

An unpolished people, it is observed, have little or no curiosity, I had seated myself by the fire-side in one of the houses at Harlech without the inhabitants expressing the least surprize at it; the Guide and attendants began to be rather clamorous for some refreshment, and the people at length brought them some oat meal bread, four porter, and stinking cheese. On my leaving the house, I believe I gave the mistress of it more than she expected, for the immediately recalled me to share some cockles with her, that were stewing on the hearth, and whilst I was tasting them, she super-added a look of such native kindness and good-will, as infinitely surpassed all the artifices of refinement.

From Harlech a fresh guide conducted me over the top of the mountain, and I found an entire good road on my return to Tan y Bwlch.

Leaving my little Inn there with regret, I passed a dreary cloud-capt country, till I came to a road which, for near a mile, was cut through a barren rock, and finely preparative for the scene that was to open upon me. On a sudden I came upon Pont Aber-glaflyn, the bridge that divides the counties of Merioneth and Carnarvon. It consists of only one wide stone arch, thrown over a considerable waterfall, from two perpendicular precipices; beyond it is a semicircle of rock, which forms a salmon leap, above which, in spawning time, the fish frequently attempt to lodge themselves, at the amazing height of five or six yards; they are frequently caught here in the season with nets, and sometimes with spears that are barbed for the purpose; but having passed the bridge, how shall I express my feelings!—the dark tremendous precipices, the rapid river roaring over disjointed rocks, black caverns, and issuing cataracts,—all serve to make this the noblest specimen of the Finely Horrid, the eye can possibly behold,—the Poet has not described, nor the Painter pictured so gloomy a retreat, 'tis the last Approach to the mansion of Pluto through the regions of Despair.

Having staid too long in contemplating this amazing pass, I posted as fast as possible over a rocky desert to gain some refreshment at Bethkelert; the blacksmith's house appearing the neatest, I alighted, and was able to obtain two eggs, which might here be considered as a most luxurious repast. At Tan y Bwlch I had been informed, that I should really meet with very decent accommodations at Bettus, and might with comfort take up my abode there for an evening. As I travelled, I reflected on Burnet's Description of a part of Carnarvonshire, that it was "the fragment of a demolished world," and on making some flight observation to the Guide of the dreariness that surrounded me, "Aye, master, says he, this must have been an ancient country indeed, for you see it is worn out to the very stones," this remark however, is probably rather good than new;—but we were now arrived at Bettus, and the Guide pointed to the house, where I hit was to get lodging and entertainment;—the violent stench did do not prevent my looking in,—the savages sat lapping their oatmeal and milk, and the swine were attendant at the table. In such a situation, only one question could properly be asked, which to was, how many miles to Carnarvon? Finding the distance only six miles, I determined to hazard being lost in the night, rather than to be suffocated in this nauseous dungeon. I must own I did here expatiate a little on recommendations, and said it was impossible that the Guide, as well as the mistress of the Inn at Tan y Bwlch, could be so intolerably mistaken; the man apologized with great frankness, that he did not think the house altogether so bad, as my Honour would have been sure to have gotten some good ale;—however, a midst all my vexation, I could not help doubting, whether Man sunk into a Savage at Bettus, or polished into an Ape at Paris, was altogether the more respectable animal.

Within three miles of Carnarvon I was agreeably surprised with a very fine road, and a new Bridge, which will open a free communication with these unfrequented regions, and induce the Curious to visit the Wonders of the British Alps, in preference to the Mountains of Switzerland, or the Glaciers of Savoy.—Mr. Barrington, who, to a consummate knowledge in the formation of Laws, adds Zeal and Propriety in the execution of them, has now indicted all the parishes between Carnarvon and Bethkelert; and indeed, unless men of great rank, or the justices of each district, will take upon them this office, that Bill, which was in many parts so excellently framed by Mr. Gilbert about two years ago, must become totally void and inefficacious;—I know that it will be immediately said, that any private gentleman has the same means within his own power; but what private gentleman, for the sake of a road, will live in perpetual warfare with five or six parishes around him?—Who, for the convenience of rolling his carriage a quarter of an hour sooner to some neighbouring market-town, will endanger his plantations being cut down, or his cattle to be either maimed or destroyed?

I passed my evening at a very good inn at Carnarvon, and having procured an intelligent Guide, returned early next morning through Bettus to the foot of Snowdon.—Having left my horses at a small hut, and hired a mountaineer to carry some cordials and provisions, with a spiked stick, but imprudently without nails in my shoes, about ten o'clock I began to ascend the mountain.—The two first miles, were rather boggy and disagreeable, but when the prospect opened, I soon forgot all difficulties;—in the course of the two last I passed by fix precipices, which I believe were very formidable, but as I was near the brink, and the wind very high, I did not venture to examine too narrowly.—On the summit, which is a plain about six yards in circumference, the air was perfectly mild and serene, and I could with pleasure contemplate the amazing map that was unfolded to my view. From hence may be distinctly seen, Wicklow Hills in Ireland, the Isle of Man, Cumberland, Lancashire, Cheshire, Shropshire, and part of Scotland;—all the counties of North Wales, the Isle of Anglesea;—rivers, plains, woods, rocks, and mountains, fix and twenty lakes, and two seas;—it is doubted whether there is an other circular prospect so extensive in any part of the terraqueous globe. Who could take such a Survey, without perceiving his Spirits elevated in some proportion to the Height?— Who could behold so bountiful a Display of Nature without Wonder and Ecstasy? Who but must feel even a Degree of Pride from having gained an eminence, from which he could with ease overlook the Nest[6] of the Eagle, and the Nest of the Hawk?

But as the level walks of Life are best suited to the generality of Mankind, it became necessary to consider that this was no spot where I could properly make any lasting Abode, and that the Return would be attended with at least as much difficulty as the Ascent.——Having descended a mile

---

6   Moel Guidon, and Moel Happock, two mountains near Snowdon, mentioned by Lord Lyttelton.
      Vide *Account of a Journey into Wales.*

or two, I did not think it amiss to enquire about an exhausted Mine that I saw at a distance; and I could make this enquiry with the better grace, as the Guides had hitherto quite wondered at my prowess; the Mine I was informed was only Copper; and happy was it for the Welsh that their Mines did not consist of choicer Metals; had they been cursed with either Gold or Silver, Foreign Nations long since, in the name of the God of Peace, and under pretence of teaching them an immaculate Religion,[7] had laid waste their country, and murdered its inhabitants.

At the Foot of Snowdon I turned about half a mile out of the way to see a Waterfall;—the Side-rock was exceedingly beautiful, but the Cataract itself was rather contemptible, after the noble ones I had seen in the neighbourhood of Dolgelly.—As the Guides seemed to think a floating island, about two miles distant, was a most wonderful phænomenon, and related many sin-

---

7   The Spaniards made the Gospel an Excuse for all the barbarities they committed in the conquest of Peru, and when they plundered the rich mines of Potosi, they frequently (says Las Casas) erected gibbets all over the country, and hung twelve poor wretches at a time, in honour of the twelve Apostles.

gular and surprising tales concerning it, I indulged their credulity so far as to go and inspect it;—the Lake, as they called it, was some what bigger than a common duck-pond; and the Island was a knotty piece of Bog, which, after very heavy rains, might very possibly float in it.

On my return to Carnarvon I examined the Town and Castle. The town was built by the command of Edward the First, out of the ruins of the ancient city of Segontium, that stood a little be low it; it is situated between two rivers, and has a beautiful prospect of the Isle of Anglesea;—it was formerly of very great account when the Princes of Wales kept their Chancery and Exchequer Courts there. On the west side of it stands the Castle, which was built to curb the Welsh mountaineers, and secure a passage to the opposite shore—In a part of it, called the Eagle Tower, you are shewn the remains of a chamber in which Edward the Second[8] is said to have been born about ten years after

---

8   The Cradle of that weak, wicked, unfortunate prince is still preserved; it is now in the possession of a clergyman in Gloucestershire, to whom it descended from one of his ancestors, who attended the Prince in his infancy.

his birth it was besieged by the Welsh, but was afterwards repaired; and both the town and castle had divers Privileges confirmed to them by different Sovereigns, down to the reign of Elizabeth; during the last civil war they were held for King Charles, but were after wards surrendered on conditions to the Parliament. On viewing these spacious Ruins, I could only ruminate on the Changes they had undergone;—strange Reverse!—to think that those Walls, which heretofore resounded with Acclamations on the Birth of the first English Prince of Wales, should now afford Shelter only to a few miserable Cottages, from the tempestuous Blasts of the Bristol channel!

I made several Excursions into the Isle of Anglesea, the well known Seat of the Druids;[9]—this may now be considered as Classical Ground; for though Mona is destroyed, and her Altars abolished, though Fires have consumed her Groves, and her Priests have perished by the Sword, yet,

---

9   For an extensive treatment of this theory, see Henry Rowlings *Mona Antiqua Restaurata* (Dublin: Aaron Rhames, 1723); a modern hardcover edition, based on the second, corrected and improved edition of 1766, was published by Hounskull in 2023. —Ed.

like the Phoenix, she rises more glorious from Decay; her Ashes have given Birth to the Caractacus of Mason, and the Fate of her Bards to the Inspiration of Gray.

Nothing could be more delightful than the Ride from Carnarvon to Bangor; to the right hand were Snowdon Hills, and to the left the River Menai, or more properly speaking, the Strait between the Continent and the Island of Anglesea; I had now got into Day-light and the polite World again; there had been a Diversion the night before at Carnarvon, and the road was covered over with Carriages.

Bangor lies at the north end of the same Frith, or arm of the Sea, which is the passage to Anglesea, where it has a Harbour for Boats. It was once so large as to be called Bangor the Great, and was defended with a powerful Castle, built by Hugh Earl of Chester,[10] which has long since been demolished. The Town is now of very little Note, except for being the See of a Bishop; the Palace is neat, but deplorably situated;—this is doubly mortifying in a Coun-

---

10   In around 1080. —Ed.

try where every part of the neighbourhood is picturesque and pleasing; his Lordship however has the happiness of being so much beloved in his Diocese, that it would have been almost Treason there to have wished him a Removal.

Between Bangor and Conway I passed over the famous Mountain called Penmaen Mawr—the road must formerly have been very frightful, but a Wall is now built to the Sea side, to which it is said the City of Dublin very largely contributed;—to form this road it has already cost upwards of two thousand pounds, and it can be kept open only at a continual expence, for vast Fragments of Rock are frequently falling forty fathom from above, which entirely block it up, till they are forced through the Parapet into the Sea, which lies perpendicularly full as deep below.[11]

From hence the Country opens into a Plain, which extends as far as the River Conway, the eastern Limit of the County of Carnarvon. It rises out of a Lake of the same

---

11 This walled road, as the author might have seen it, can be seen depicted in the c. 1835 engraving by W. Radclyffe, *Penmaen Mawr*, after D. Cox. —Ed.

name, and runs with a north-west Course,
receiving in the short space of twelve miles
more than as many Rivers, so that at Aber-
conway, where it discharges its waters into
the Irish Sea, its full a mile broad, and ca-
pable of bringing Ships of almost any Size
up to the Town; at present Conway bears
only some melancholy Marks of what it
once was, and to what a wretched State, by
a total Decay of Trade, it is now reduced.

The Castle still remains one of the noblest Monuments of Antiquity; it is built in
the same Style with that of Carnarvon, but
is far more regular. The Outside is the same
as in the time of Edward the First, except
one Tower, and that was not demolished
with either battering engines or cannons,
but by the people of the place taking Stones
from the foundation of it. Some Remains of
the principal Rooms are still to be seen, the
Dimensions of which have been accurate-
ly given by Lord Lyttelton, and an elegant
View of them in *Antiquities* by Mr. Grose;[12]
but I had never seen the Outside of this
most venerable Ruin to advantage had I not

12   Francis Grose, *The Antiquities of England and Wales*, 4 vols.
     (London: Hooper and Wigstead, 1773). —Ed.

walked over some polished Ground about a quarter of a mile from it, which I believe belongs to a Gentleman of Conway;—there You see the Castle finely sheltered by an Oak Wood,—on one side the *Chief of Rivers* opening into the Irish Sea, and on the other the Mountains surrounding Penmaen, with a distant Country most beautifully diversified.—Art and Nature cannot combine to form a more various and more delicious Prospect.

I could not possibly leave this part of the Country without feeing the Vale of Llanryst, the Bridge built by Inigo Jones, and the Chapel supposed to have been planned by him, which contains the rich monuments of the Guedir Family.[13]—The Vale upon the whole I thought inferior to that I had seen in Montgomeryshire, but the Bridge is certainly a very elegant Structure, and speaks itself to be the Work of a great Architect, most probably of Jones, for I incline to the opinion that Llanryst was the Place of his Nativity.[14]

---

13 For early accounts of this family, see Thomas Rowland, *History of the Gwydir Family* (1669) and Sir John Wynn, *The History of the Gwydir Family* (Oswestry: Woodall and Venables, 1878). —Ed.

14 Inigo Jones was born in Smithfield, London. Some sources say

The Chapel which adjoins the Parish Church, was erected by Sir Richard Wynne, one of the Grooms of the Bedchamber to Charles the First when Prince of Wales, and was chiefly made use of for the Alms-House in the neighbourhood, which was endowed by the Guedir Family. I took the Pains of copying the different Inscriptions in it, and as they are not contained in the History of that Family lately published, they may not be unacceptable to the curious Antiquary.

> This Cappel was erected Anno Domini 1633. By Sir Richard Wynne of Gwydir in the County of Carnavon Knight and Baronet, Treasurer to the High and Mighty Princess Henrietta Maria Queen of England, Daughter to King Henery the Fourth King of France, and Wife to our Soveraing King Charles. Where lieth Buried his Father St John Wynne of Gwydir in the County of Caernarvon Knight and Baronet, Son and Heyre to Maurice Wynne, Son and Heyre to John Wynne, Son and Heyre to Mer-

---

he was born in Wales, and was originally called Ynir, or Ynyr, but there are no known contemporary records corroborating these claims. —Ed.

edith, Which Three lye Buried in the Church of Dolwyddelan with Tombes over them. This Meredith Son and Heyre to Evan, Son and Heyre to Robert, Son and Heyre to Meredith, Son and Heyre to Howel, Son and Heyre to David, Son and Heyre to Griffith, Son and Heyre to Carradock, Son and Heyre to Thomas, Son and Heyre to Roderick Lord of Anglesey, Son to Owen Gwynedd Prince of Wales, and younger to David Prince of Wales, who married Eme Plantagenet Sister to King Henery the Second. There succeeded this David Three Princes, His Nephew Leolinus Magnus, who married Jone Daughter to King John, David his Son, Nephew to King Henery the Third, and Leoline the Last Prince of Wales of that House and Line who lived in King Edward the First his time. St John Wynne married Sydney who lieth buried here, the Daughter of Sr William Gerrard Knight, Lord Chancellour of Ireland, by whom he had Issue St John Wynne who died att Lucca in Italy. S Richard Wynne now living, Thomas Wynne who Lieth here, Roger Wynne who Lieth here, William Wynne now living, Maurice Wynne now living, Ellis Wynne who lieth Buried att Whitford in the County of Flint, Henery

Wynne now liveing, Roger Wynne who lieth here, and Two Daughters, Mary now living married to S[r] Roger Mostyn in the County of Flint Knight. and Elizabeth now liveing married to S[r] John Bodvil in the County of Caernarvon Knight.

On the Floor are four Brass Plates, with Drawings of Figures upon each of them in the Dresses of the Times, one of Maria Mostyn, Wife of Roger Mostyn, another of Sir Owen Wynne, an other of Sir John Wynne, and a Fourth of Lady Sydney Wynne, Wife of Sir John Wynne. And in the Corner of the Chapel a Stone Coffin, which was removed from the Abbey of Conway, about two miles from hence, on which is the following Inscription:

This is the Coffin of Leolinus Magnus Prince of Wales who was buried in the Abbey of Conway, and upon the Dissolution, remov'd from thence.

On each Side are six carved Recesses in the figure of Flower de Luces, which bear evident Marks of having contained Brass

Plates, and two at the bottom of the Coffin.

There is now erected in the Church a Gallery of exquisite Workmanship, which was removed likewise from the Abbey; and I was at the trouble of having a large quantity of Rubbish taken away from under an old Staircase, that I might inspect a Stone Effigy, which is said to be of Hoel Coetmore,[15] who sold the Guedir Estate to the Wynne Family; the Word Gwedir is supposed to signify Glass, and that Family probably was the first who in these parts had a House with glazed Windows.

I ought to make some Apology for the foregoing heavy Articles, but elaborate Inscriptions frequently illustrate History, and These will at least shew that Some of the Welsh were not totally regardless of Pedigree.

I made diligent through all Carnarvonshire, and this part of Denbighshire, for the Glyder Mountain, which Gibson has particularly described, and which, from its singularity, (say the Authors of a *Tour through Wales*,) we more wished to have

---

15   It was his son, Dafydd, who sold the estate to Maredudd ab Ieuan ab Robert (d. 1525) in around 1500. —Ed.

seen, than the Summits of either Plinlimmon or Snowdon.

On the utmost top of this Mountain,
according to the Continuator of Camden, who saw it, is a prodigious pile of
Stones, many of which are of the mag-
nitude of those at Stonehenge. They lie
in such an irregular manner, crossing
and supporting each other, that some
people have imagined them to be the
remains of a vast building; but Gibson
more naturally supposes them to be the
skeleton or ruins of the Mountain; the
weaker parts of which may have been
worn away in a series of ages, by the
rains and meltings of the Snow.

On the west side of the fame mountain, he speaks of a remarkable preci-
pice, adorned with numerous equidis-
tant columns, formed to that shape by
the almost continual rains, which this
high rock, being exposed to the westerly
sea wind, is subject to.

Notwithstanding the situation of this
mountain seems to be pointed out by
the last line, and though its Phænome-
na are so peculiar, yet We (add the Authors of the same Tour) were obliged to
leave the Country, without gaining the
smallest knowledge of it.

I was equally unfortunate in not being able to see this Mountain, but in crossing the wide Ferry at Conway, I by accident gained such Information, that I am confident any future Traveller may very readily satisfy his Curiosity; an old Boatman there informed me, that he had frequently seen it, that in his younger days indeed it was some times termed the Glyder, but was now known only by the name of Wythwar,—that it was within a mile or two of a Village, called Clynog, and upon the Shore almost opposite to Carnarvon.

On my way to St. Asaph, I passed over the top of Penmaen Ross, a steep and formidable Mountain; this is by far the worst part of the road between Holyhead and Chester;—a nearer Path was some time since cut along the side of the sea cliff, but a Man and Horse had lately been killed, and by order of the Commissioners it is now entirely broken up.

The City of St. Asaph is called in British Llan Elwy, on account of its situation at the Conflux of the River Elwy with the Clwyd; and St. Asaph by the English, from its Patron Asaph, who in the year 560 erected a

Bishop's See there. The Bishop of this Diocese has no entire County under his Jurisdiction, but Parts only of the Counties of Flint, Denbigh, Montgomery, Merioneth, and Salop. The Cathedral is a mean Structure, and the Houses in general but ill built, St. Asaph however may boast that it stands in the delightful Vale of Clwyd, though by no means in the finest part of it.

About five miles from thence, near the road to Holywell, You have the best View I think of that fertile and delicious Vale;—it is of an oval shape, about 25 miles in length, and about eight miles wide in its broadest part; it lies open only to the Ocean, and to the clearing North Wind, being elsewhere guarded with high mountains, which towards the East especially are like Battlements or Turrets, for by an admirable Contrivance of Nature, says Camden, the tops of these Mountains resemble the Turrets of Walls. Upon the whole however I think that there are other cultivated Scenes in North Wales equal, if not superior; in the Vale of Clwyd indeed You have the Lively and the Beautiful, but in Montgomeryshire the Awful and Sublime.

Holywell, and the History of its Virgin Saint, would require at least a Folio. I shall only say that I was truly sorry to find that blasphemous Papers should still be suffered to be publicly sold at the Spring there, which compare the ludicrous Legend of Winefrid with the most sacred Truths of the Gospel.

It was my Intention to have seen Winstay, Erthig, and Chirk Castle,[16] and afterwards to have traced the River Dee to Bala, but I was unexpectedly called off from my Tour; I had the good fortune however to join Party with the Bishop of Kildare,[17] whose easy Manners and refined Conversation left me no room to regret a Disappointment.

To the foregoing Account, which was in part printed off for the Use and Amusement of some select Friends only, I shall now add a few general Remarks on the History of the Country and the Manners of its Inhabitants.

The Origin of every Nation is necessarily obscure, and always lost in a pretend-

---

16   Sir Watkin Wynne's, Mr. Yorke's, and Mr. Middleton's.

17   At this time, Charles Jackson, who held the post from 1765 until his death in 1790. —Ed.

ed Antiquity. On the Authority of Bochart we may trace the Welsh from Japhet, the Son of Noah; according to Others, from Trojans and Phœnicians, who were the Offspring of Gods; and one Writer I think has asserted that a True Briton is a Compound of all Nations under Heaven. That Britain however was peopled from Gaul 1000 years before Christ, appears very probable,—the arguments in favour of this opinion are deduced from the State of Population on the Continent, and from the Progress of it in the Island itself. It has been well observed[18] that Names descriptive of national Manners cannot be the original Appellations of any people, they result from the intercourse and experience of the States around them, on whose territories they have dared to encroach; the Appellation of Brigantes, according to Strabo, came to signify a turbulent and plundering race, and the Denominations of Celtæ and Gael came to import, even amongst themselves, the Ferocious and the Stranger.

---

18   By Whitaker.

The Name of Cymri appears to have been the great hereditary Distinction of the Gauls upon the Continent, and to have been carried with them into all their Conquests; it was not retained in our Island merely by the Natives of Wales, but was equally the Appellation of a Nation in the South-West of Somersetshire and the North-East of Cornwall.

The first Denomination of our Island was certainly Albion, a name given before the Country was inhabited; it was the Celtic Term for Heights or Eminences; the Alps some ages before the Days of Strabo were called Albia, and in his time there remained two tribes on the Mountains that bore the Names of Albiœci, and Albienses.

The second Denomination was that of Britain, derived from a Celtic Word likewise dignifying *Divided*, not *Painted*; this Etymology has lately been proved not to have been applied to the Region, but bestowed on the Inhabiters; not previously borne on the Continent by the original Settlers of the Country, but assumed or received at their first Removal into the Island.

The Title of Welsh seems to arise from the Word Wall or Gall, an appellation which the Britons frequently gave each other; nor will this Derivation appear forced if we add, that the Channel betwixt France and England was denominated Sinus Vallicus, or the Gallick Strait, so late as the eighth Century, and that the Dutch and Germans call the French by the Name of Walls and Walloons to this very Day.

The general Denomination of Wales was not imposed on the Country by the Saxons, but was the acknowledged Appellation of the Region as early as the sixth Century, if we may believe a Quotation from Taliessin, as cited by Dr. Davies.

Nor were some plain and certain Derivations of Names till of late only unknown to us,—we have not always had either just Ideas of British Manners or British Antiquities; this ample Field of History has been greatly laid open by an Individual,[19] and a rich Produce will continually arise from the judicious Publications of a most respectable Society.[20]

Our Knowledge of the Druids is still vague and unsatisfying, and must ever re-

19   Whitaker.

20   Society of Antiquaries [of London. —Ed.]

main so, as they committed few things, if any, to Writing, though they were certainly not unacquainted with Letters; for among the Maxims collected by Gollet, there is one that forbids their Mysteries to be written, a Prohibition which could never have been given had Letters been entirely unknown; some curious Particulars however may at least be traced from Tradition, and others from Specimens of their Poetry that have been recited by the Natives. As Guardians of what They called True Religion, they of course possessed the greatest authority among the people; No Laws were institut-ed by the Princes without their Advice, no Plunder taken in War without their partak-ing of it. They held the Dissolution of the World by Fire and Water, they taught the Immortality, and some say the Transmigra-tion of the Soul, a Doctrine borrowed from the Pythagoreans, though Clemens Alexan-drinus expressly asserts that the Pythago-reans borrowed that Doctrine from them; in my own opinion they never believed the Transmigration of the Soul at all; and I found this opinion on some late Accounts of Gaulish Funerals, which certainly corresponded with the British ones; the Customs and Ceremonials of which were absolutely incompatible with that Doctrine.

They sacrificed human Victims to propitiate the Gods; and prophesied future Events from the falling of the Body, and the Manner in which the Members were convulsed;—they believed there was a divine Mystery in Misleto, but took their first Distinction from the Oak, to which the Jews paid the same regard during their Idolatry, according to a Passage in Ezekiel, "under every thick *Oak* did they offer sweet Sacrifice to their Idols." Once a year They, with their Chief, an Arch-Druid, assembled at a fixed time and place to hear Causes, and determine all Disputes; where their decisive Court was held has never been determined, but most probably in Anglesea, as that Island was certainly their Metropolis. So great was the Power of the Druids, that not only the Property, but also the Lives of the People were entirely at their Disposal, and this Power continued absolute till the time of Tiberius;—it was afterwards suppressed by Claudius, under the fair Pretext of abolishing human sacrifices, but the

Priests themselves, their Gods and their Altars subsisted, though in obscurity, till the final Destruction of Paganism.

The Manners of the People were naturally tinged with the Discipline of their Teachers; in proportion to their ignorance they were superstitious, and in proportion to their zeal they committed Cruelties and Fraud; I shall not raise Disgust by a recital of Barbarities, but rather refer my Readers to the Journals of modern Voyages, where they will find, that there is a Sameness in the primæval State of every savage Nation: a few other Particulars however may not be uninteresting. The Britons lived in Tribes or Clans, under the Aristocratical rule of their several Lords; their Villages were a confused Parcel of Huts placed at a small distance from each other, and, generally speaking, in the middle of a Wood, whereof the Avenues were defended with Trees, that were cut down to clear the ground.

Their Trade was very inconsiderable, notwithstanding the convenient situation of the Island for carrying on an extensive Commerce; Their vessels were very small, with their Keels and Ribs made of slight

Timber, interwoven with Wicker, and covered with Hides, which shews that they never undertook long Voyages, most probably never ventured to Sea beyond the Coasts of Gaul.

The Britons were not so totally destitute of Defence as has been imagined; the Island is of itself a Shield, and they certainly made use of the Battle-axe, as well as Military Chariot; these Chariots were drawn by Horses, and the Axle-trees were generally furnished with Scythes; but the People were not united under a well regulated government, or they would always have continued formidable to their Enemies; a number of petty Communities will never act in concert with each other; tho' History informs us that upon great and extraordinary Dangers a Chief Commander was always chosen by common consent; but what State or Colony will acquiesce even with the Leader themselves have chosen? and in the end, if unsuccessful, he must always fall a Sacrifice to those Miseries their own Inconsistencies alone have occasioned.

When that part of Britain' which comprehends the present Kingdom of England

and Principality of Wales, was divided into several petty Kingdoms, the Inhabitants were all distinguished by different names. The Principality of Wales, formerly comprehending the whole Country beyond the Severn, was in the Roman times occupied by the Silures, the Dimetæ, and Ordovices; to these belonged not only the twelve Counties of Wales, but likewise the two others lying beyond the Severn, Herefordshire and Monmouthshire, which in the reign of Charles the Second were first reckoned amongst the English Counties.

The Country now known by the name of North Wales was inhabited by the Ordovices only, who held out first against the Romans, and afterwards against the English, after the other Britons were subdued; for by the Romans they were not reduced till the time of Domitian, nor by the English till the Reign of Henry the First.

About forty-five years before the Christian Era, Britain was first invaded by the Romans under Julius Cæsar,—afterwards by Claudius, and at length became a Province under the Roman empire; it was governed by Lieutenants, or Deputies, sent from Rome, as

Ireland is now by Deputies from England; and continued thus under the Romans for upwards of 400 years; till that Empire being invaded by the Goths and Vandals, the Romans were forced not only to recall their own armies, but also to draw from hence the bravest of the Britons, for their assistance against those Barbarians.

The Country being left in a defenceless State, was invaded by the Scots, who were so rapacious, that the Britons sent over a miserable application for relief to Erius, the Roman General, who by several famous, Successes, for a time, had repelled the violence of the Gothick Arms, but receiving no hopes of any Succours from that General, the South Britons invited over the Saxons, who no sooner delivered them from their ancient Foes the Picts and Scots, than they strengthened their own Numbers, turned their Arms against the Natives, and conquered them, some few excepted, who secured themselves in the Mountains of Wales; whence their Descendants have always been distinguished by the Title of Ancient Britons.

During the Saxon Heptarchy lived the renowned Prince Arthur, whose Valour would have retrieved the miserable state of the Britons, had Valour only been wanting his History has been so blended with Fable, that some have doubted the real existence of such a Person; but it seems rather hard because Stories have been invented concerning the Actions of his Life, that he should not be allowed to have lived at all; it is true that the Saxon Annals make no mention of this King, but it was not probable that the Saxons would be fond of recording Exploits, which redounded only to their own discredit; an ancient English Historian speaking of Cerdic, mentions his fighting several Battles with King Arthur; and William of Malmesbury owns, that though the Britons had vented innumerable Fables concerning this Prince, he certainly was a Hero worthy to be celebrated in True History. The Britons bewailed "their long loft Arthur" for several Ages after his Death;—they believed he was still alive in Fairy Land, and that he would return once more to reign over them nor was this notion rooted out till the reign of Henry the Second, about six hundred years after wards, when his Coffin was dug up at Glastenbury in Somersetshire, with the following Inscription, "Here lies buried the renowned King Arthur in the Island Avalonia." The Exploits of this Warrior have not not only been sung by Taliessin and other British Bards, but have been celebrated by one of the greatest of our English Poets; it seems by some Hints given by Spenser, that he intended a Poem whose title was to be expressly, King Arthur;—Dryden tells us that he had some thoughts of making choice for the subject of an Heroic Poem, King Arthur's Conquests over the Saxons; Milton, in a Latin Address to Mansus, has likewise intimated the same Intention.

Wales was anciently bounded by the Irish Seas, and by the Rivers Severn and Dee till the Saxons became Masters of all the level Countries over those Rivers; and till Offa, king of Mercia, made the celebrated Trench, which is still called by his Name. This Trench, which extended from North to South, from the mouth of the River Dee to that of the Wye, has been thought to have been an Imitation of the Ramparts, which were thrown up by Agricola, Adrian, and Severus, to guard the Romans against the Incursions of the Northern Barbarians; but from some Remains of it, as well as for several other Reasons, it seems more probable, that it was not intended by Offa as a Fortification, but rather as a Boundary betwixt his Kingdom and the Cambrian Province.

When after many Events between the several Races of the Heptarchy, Ecbert became the sole King of England, as it was now distinguished from the Principality of Wales, he possessed himself also of Mona, the Capital of the Cambrian Province; but the Saxons some time afterwards being driven out of it, it was from them called Anglesea, Englishman's Island, a name which it has retained ever since.

In the year eight hundred and forty-three all Wales was united under the Dominion of Roderic, surnamed the Great; who, by a testamentary Settlement, made a new Division between three Sons into three Districts, which were called Kingdoms, and distinguished by the Names of South Wales, Powis Land, and North Wales rise to many this Partition gave rife to Wars, which caused the Kingdom of Powis Land to be portioned among the Conquerors, and annexed partly to South Wales, and partly to North Wales, Divisions which subsist to this Day.

No sooner were the Saxons settled under one Monarch, than the Danes began to trouble them, as they (the Saxons) had before done the Britons, till, after many Invasions, Edgar King of England set forth the first Navy, made Peace with the Danes, and allowed them to live in his Dominions mixed with the English;—at this time we read of five Kings in Wales, who all did him Homage for their Country.

Notwithstanding many Attempts of the English, the Welsh enjoyed their own Laws, and lived under their own Princes, till in the year 1282 Llewellin lost both his Principality and Life; in the reign of Henry the Eighth Wales was incorporated and united with England; and by a Statute of the 27th of that Reign, all Laws and Liberties of England were to take place there; from which time the Welsh have approved themselves truly worthy of their high Origin, loyal and dutiful to their King, and always zealous for the Welfare of the Community.

The Welsh Language is still the Gomerian or Old Celtic, the fame that was once spoken throughout Europe, except that through length of time, and Intermixture of the people with the Scythians and other nations, it has split into a variety of Dialects. No Tongue, either ancient or modern, I believe, bears greater Marks of antiquity; its strong resemblance to the Hebrew has been generally admitted, insomuch that one Author of great Learning has given a Specimen of a considerable number of Phrases out of the Old Testament, which are so alike in both, that they seem to have been originally the same. It is no uncommon Error to give the Name of Mother Tongue to those Languages, from which some known Idioms only are derived; the Hebrew has been considered as a Mother Tongue, but was evidently borrowed from the Phœnician; the Latin is called the Mother tongue to the Italian, the Spanish, and the French, but the Latin itself was derived from the Tuscan, and the Tuscan from the Celtic and the Greek. It will reasonably be asked, how the Gomerians have preserved their Language almost entire, whilst the Jews have suffered theirs to be corrupted, and blended with those of their Conquerors?—for this, many reasons may be assigned; the Former have not been so frequently subdued, and they have always preserved a considerable Regard for what They conceived to be a Mother tongue; a regard greatly kept up perhaps by the Custom which the Lowest of the People had, of reciting their Genealogies. This ancient Language is spoken the nearest to its original purity in the uncultivated parts of North Wales, but the Welsh in general still retain so high a veneration for it, that I am confident they will never readily suffer the English to be entirely made use of in their Churches, or taught solely in their Schools.

Much has been said of those Druidical Remains, which by many Authors have been indiscriminately called Carns, Carnedds, and Cromlechs; but of their original meaning, I shall venture the following Conjecture, that by the word Carn, which signified a Rock, the Britons simply implied one large broad Stone, as a covering for a Grave;[21] by

---

21 The Word Carn was afterwards used in an ill sense, most probably when the Mode of Burial came to be changed on the Introduction of Christianity; then Malefactors being thrown into holes near the Highways, and great quantities of Stones heaped upon them, it was no uncommon thing for a man to say

a Carnedd, a heap of Stones thrown rude-
ly together to commemorate an event; and
by a Cromlech, an huge, broad, flat Stone
raised high on other Stones, where the ancient Britons, like the Hebrews, made Sacrifices or paid religious Adoration.

Those nice Distinctions that have been
formed of the Druids, the Bards and the
Vates, subsisted only, I think, in particular
Societies; the Druids in general composed
and recited Hymns, as worship to their
Deities; the Bards[22] certainly composed
Hymns likewise; but it was in the hour of
Battle that their labours were chiefly cele-
brated, by singing the Exploits of deceased
Heroes; while the Vates were principally
engaged in the Rites of Sacrifice, or the Arts
of Divination.

---

to his enemy; *May a Carn be your Monument.*

22 The Bards, who were inferior Druids, wore an ecclesiastical
Ornament during the celebration of their Rites, called by the
Latins Caputium, or Cucullus, which is still retained in our
Universities; the Gauls, who borrowed this custom from the
British Druids, wore the Cucullus remarkably long, whence it
obtained, on its being made use of at Rome, the name of Bar-
do-Cucullus, or Bard's Hood. It was in allusion to the Shape of
this Hood, that Martial feared left a Sheet of his Book should
be rolled up to put Pepper or Frankincense in:
Ne Thuris Piperisve sit Cucullus.
VID. NICHOLLS.

The Welsh have always laid claim to the Discovery of America, in preference to the Great Columbus, but this claim has hither to been supported with little more than bare Conjecture; in the twelfth Century, according to Powell, there was a War in Wales for the Succession, upon the Death of Owen Guinneth; and a Bastard having carried it from the lawful Heirs, one of the latter, called Madoc, put to Sea, and failing west from Spain, discovered a new world of wonderful Fertility to prove that a country was thus discovered, the Welsh have recourse to the Authority of Meridith ap Rhees, who composed an Ode in honour Prince Madoc and his new-found Land; and that this Country was America they have alledged on the credit of Peter Martyr, that the Natives of Virginia celebrated the memory of one Madoc, as a great and ancient Hero; and always supposed their Ancestors to have come thither at first, from some very distant Countries on the other side the great Water, at the time that has been asserted, and from the same point of the Compass. The affinity of Language has since been frequently urged by modern Travellers, and Bishop Nicholson in particular, speaks confidently that the British makes a considerable part of several of the American Tongues; in answer to these Assertions, the ingenious Dr. Robertson has just now declared, that he conceives the skill of the Welsh in the twelfth Century, not to have been equal to such a Voyage; and that the instances given of the affinity of Language are so obscure and fanciful, that no conclusion can be drawn from them; to these remarks he adds, that if the Welsh towards the Close of the twelfth Century had fettled in any part of America, some remains of the Christian doctrine must have been afterwards found among their Descendants, when they were discovered three hundred years after their migration;—but here I must entirely disagree with the learned Author,—three hundred years cannot in this case be called a "short period;"—one Century would probably have been sufficient to have obliterated every mark of a Religion, that had to combat with the prejudices of an unlettered people; that did not address itself immediately to their Interests, and through a Mode of Civilization, teach them at first only, as Warburton well expresses it,[23] the emollient Arts of Life.

Christianity seems to have been introduced into Britain, as early as the first Century, but of this great Event our Accounts must necessarily be very imperfect, as the Saxons destroyed almost all the Writings in which it was recorded; Mona, we read, had certainly a School of Christian Learning many years before 182, when there was an Archbishop of Caerleon, and Suffragans under him; but the Clergy had no distinct Parishes either in Anglesea or any other part of the kingdom, till many years afterwards. About the year 600, Pope Gregory sent Austin the Monk to preach the Gospel in England to the Heathen Saxons, who was received by Ethelbert; and being admitted to explain the Doctrine and Mysteries of it, so well succeeded that he converted great numbers, and at length the King himself.

---

23 The Gospel, plain and simple as it is, and fitted in its nature for what it was ordained to effect, requires an intellect something above that of a Savage to apprehend. Nor is it at all to the dishonour of our holy Faith, that such a one must be taught a previous lesson; and first of all instructed in the emollient *Arts of Life*. See the Bishop of Gloucester's *Sermon on the Propagation of the Gospel* .

Thus the Christian Religion came to be established in England under the Rites and Authority of the Romish Church, by which Austin was instituted Chief Bishop, and seated by the Saxon king at Canterbury; but his Jurisdiction, though admitted in all the Saxon Territories, was not received by the British Priests or People in Wales. In the reign of Elizabeth the Bible and Common Prayer were first translated into the Welsh Tongue,[24] and at that time the People are said to have adhered to the Rubrick and Constitution of the Church with a scrupulous exactness; how far the Doctrines and Worship of Christianity may have deviated from their original purity, or how far the Welsh may have been affected by the refined Tenets of their English Neighbours, I shall not presume to determine, at present I think there is every where much to be feared, from the Growth of Enthusiasm, the subtleties of Infidelity, and the Necessity, as well as Danger of Innovation.

Many Popish customs are still retained in Wales, particularly Offerings made to

---

24   In 1588, by William Morgan (1545 - 1604), Bishop of Llandaff and St Asaph. —Ed.

the Dead, these Offerings must of course vary according to the Rank of the Persons deceased, as well as the Affection that is borne to their Memories; I was at a Pauper's Funeral where the Donations amounted to half a Crown, and I met with a Clergyman afterwards who had once received ninety Guineas.

Great complaints are made in many parts of this Country of the exorbitant Demands of Landlords, and that the Rent of Ground is now advanced much higher than it will bear;—such Complaints must of course be expected from the Sufferers, but I believe, they are here in some instances made with reason; the landlords on the contrary may urge perhaps, that they act with strict Justice, and that they have a Right at least to try the experiment; but it should be remembered that the Extreme of Right is Wrong, and there is a Tribute of Humanity due from the Superior, that He should be always on a Certainty that he does not exact too much.

National Characters should always be read with Exceptions; but if I must give my opinion of the Inhabitants of North Wales, I shall say, that the common people in general are civil and grateful, the Farmers rather slow and suspicious, a Few of the inferior Squires retain somewhat of the sottish and the brutal, but among the higher Ranks, I have found, in the same proportion as in England, lettered Society, hospitable Reception, and refined Address.

F I N I S.

Index

Æ

Æthelberht of Kent 56

A

Aberystwith Castle 16
Account of a Journey into
    Wales (Littelton) 22
Acheron 14
Agricola 48
Albienses 39
Albiœci 39
Albion 39
America 54, 55
American tongues 55
Antiquities of England and

Wales, The (Grose) 28
Arthur, King 46, 48
Augustine of Canterbury 56, 57
Avalonia 48
Avranches, Earl of Chester,
    Hugh d' 26

B

Bala 6, 37
Bangor 26, 27
Bangor Castle 26
bards 26, 48, 53
Barrington, 2nd Viscount Bar-
    rington, William 20
Barrington, Mr 20
Beddgelert 18, 20

Betws y Coed 18, 19, 20, 21
Bible, translated into Welsh 57
Bodvil, Sir John 32
Book of Common Prayer, trans-
    lated into Welsh 57
Bouverie, 1st Earl of Radnor,
    William 14
Bristol 25
Britain 2, 38, 39, 44, 45, 56
British Alps 20
Britons 40, 43, 44, 45, 46, 47,
    50, 52, 53
Burnet, Thomas 18

C

Cader 2
Cader Idris 6, 8
Caerleon, Archbishop of 56
Caernarfon 16, 17, 19, 20, 21,
    24, 26, 27, 28, 35
Caernarfon Castle 16, 24
Caernarfonshire 9, 18, 33
Cæsar, Julius 45
Cairns 52
Camden, William 34, 36
Canterbury 57
Caractacus 26
Caradog ap Rhodri ap Owain
    Gwynedd 31
Caradog ap Tomas ap Rhodri
    31
Cayne, River 12
Celts 38
Charles II of England 5, 45
Charles I of England, Scotland,
    and Ireland 25, 30
Cheshire 22
Chester 26, 35
Chirk Castle 37

Christianity 52, 56, 57
Claudius 42, 45
Clemens Alexandrinus 41
Clwyd, River 35
Clwyd, Vale of 36
Clynog 35
cock matches 8
Conwy 27, 28, 29, 32, 35
Conwy Abbey 32
Conwy Castle 15, 24, 26, 28,
    29, 37
Conwy, Llyn 27
Conwy, River 27
Cornwall 39
Cromlechs 52, 53
Cromwell, Oliver 9
Cumberland 22

D

Dafydd ab Owain 31
Dafydd ap Gruffydd 31
Dafydd ap Llywelyn 31
Danes 50
David 12
Davies, Robert (antiquary, d.
    1728) 40
Dee, River 37, 48
Denbighshire 33, 36
Derbyshire 13
Deri, Afon 11
Dimetæ 45
Dinas Mowddwy 4, 6
Dolgellau 7, 9, 10, 11, 23
Dolwyddelan 31
Domitian 45
Druidism 40
Druids 25, 40, 42, 53
Dryden, John 48
Dryryd, River 13

Dublin 9, 27
Dutchmen 40

E

Ecgberht, King of Wessex 49
Edgar, King of England 50
Edward I 16, 24, 28, 31
Edward II 24
Edward IV 16
Elizabeth, Queen of England
    and Ireland 25, 57
Elwy, River 35
England 8, 15, 30, 40, 44, 46,
    49, 50, 56, 57, 59
English Civil War 25
Englishmen 14
English, spoken 4
Erddig 37
Erius 46
Ezekiel 42

F

Flintshire 31, 36
France 30, 40
French language 51

G

Gallic Strait 40
Game Laws 6
Gaul 38, 44
Gaulish funerals 41
Gauls 39, 53
Gerard, Sir William 31
Germans 40
Gibson, Edmund 33, 34
Gilbert, Thomas 20
Glastonbury 47

Glorious Revolution 3
Gloucestershire 24
Glyder Fawr (Mountain) 33
Gomerian language 50
Gomerians 51
Goths 46
Greek language 51
Gregory I, Pope 56
Griffith, Mrs (at Tan y Bwlch)
    13
Grose, Francis 28
Gruffydd ap Caradog ap Tomas
    31
Gwydir Estate 33

H

Hadrian 48
Harlech 15, 16, 17
Harlech Castle 15, 16
Hebrew 51
Hecate (Shakespearean charac-
    ter) 14
Henrietta Maria 30
Henry I 45
Henry II 31
Henry III 31
Henry IV of France 30
Henry VIII 50
Heptarchy 46, 49
Herbert, 1st Earl of Pembroke,
    William 16
Herefordshire 45
Holyhead 35
Holywell 36, 37
human sacrifice 42
Hywel ap Dafydd 31
Hywel Coetmor 33

I

Ieuan ap Robert ap Maredudd 31
Inigo Jones Bridge 29
inns 5
Inns 11, 17, 19
Ireland 22, 31, 46
Irish Sea 15
Isle of Man 22
Italian language 51
Italy 31

J

Japhet 38
Jews 42, 51
Joan, Lady of Wales 31
John, King of England 31
John "Wynn" ap Maredudd 31
Jones, Inigo 29

K

Kedleston 13
Kildare, Bishop. *See* Jackson,
    Charles (Bishop of Kildare,
    1765 - 1790)

L

Lake of the Three Grains 9
Lancashire 22
landlords 58
Las Casas, Bartolomé de 23
La Serva Padrona (burletta) 6
Latin 48, 51
Llanfair 4
Llanrwst 29
Llanrwst, Vale of 29

Llywelyn ab Iorwerth, a.k.a.,
    Llywelyn the Great 31, 32
Llywelyn ap Gruffudd 31, 50
London 5, 6, 8
Lucca, Italy 31
Lyttelton, 1st Baron Lyttelton,
    George 3, 22, 28

M

Macbeth (Shakespearean char-
    acter) 14
Madoc ab Owain Gwynedd 54
Manso, Giovanni Battista 48
Maredudd ap Hywel ap Daffydd 31
Maredudd ap Rhys 54
Martial 53
Matlock Bath 13
Menai Strait 26
Mercia 48
Meredydd ap Ieuan ap Robert 31
Merionethshire 15, 36
military capabilities 44
Milton, John 48
Misleto 42
Moel Guidon 22
Moel Happock 22
Mona 25, 49, 56
Montgomeryshire 2, 29, 36
Morgan, William 57
Mostyn, Maria 32
Mostyn, Roger 32
Mostyn, Sir Roger 32
Mothwaye, River 12
Myddelton, Richard 37

N

national character 58
New Testament 12
Nicholson, William (Bishop) 55
Noah 38

O

Offa, King of Mercia 48, 49
Old Celtic language 50
Old Testament 12, 51
Ordovices 45
Owain Gwynedd 54

P

paganism 43
Paris 20
Parliament, House of 2, 25
Pembroke, Earl of. *See* Herbert, 1st Earl of Pembroke, William
Penmaenmawr 29
Peru 23
Peter Martyr 54
Philips, John 10
Phœnician language 51
Phœnicians 38
Picts 46
Plantagenet, Emme 31
Plinlimmon 34
Pluto 18
Pont Fawr (Inigo Jones Bridge), Llanrwst 29
Poole 4
Poor Laws 6
Potosi 23
Powell, David 54

Powis Castle 3
Powys, Kingdom of 49
Princes of Wales 24, 25, 30
Pythagoreans 41

Q

quacks 6
quarter sessions 7

R

Radnor, Lord. *See* Bouverie, 1st Earl of Radnor, William
Raffelas (Johnson) 15
rents 58
Rhaeadr Ddu / Black Cataract 14
Rhodri ab Owain Gwynedd 31
Rhodri ap Merfyn (a.k.a., Rhodri Mawr, or Rhodri the Great) 49
Robert ap Maredudd 31
Robertson, William 55
Romans 6, 45, 46, 48

S

salmon 3, 17
Salop 36
Savoy, glaciers of 20
Saxons 40, 46, 47, 48, 49, 50, 56
Scotland 22
Scots 46
Scythians 51
Segontium 24
Sermon Preached Before the Incorporated Society for the Propagation of the

Gospel in Foreign Parts, A
(Warburton) 56
Severn, River 3, 45, 48
Severus, Lucius Septimius 48
Shakespeare, William 6
Shrewsbury 2
Shropshire 22
Silures 45
Sinus Vallicus 40
Snowdon 2, 9, 21, 22, 23, 26, 34
Society of Antiquaries of London 40
Somersetshire 39, 47
South Wales xii, 49
Spain 54
Spaniards 23
Spanish language 51
Spenser, Edmund 48
St Asaph (Bishop) 35
St Asaph Cathedral 36
St Asaph, Denbighshire 35, 36
Stirom cider 10
Stonehenge 34
Strabo 38, 39
St Winefride 37
Switzerland, mountains of 20

T

Taliesin 40, 48
Tan y Bwlch 11, 12, 13, 14, 17, 18, 19
Thebes 5
Tiberius 42
trade 43
Trojans 38
Tuscan language 51

V

Vandals 46
Vates 53
Virginia 54

W

Walloons 40
Warburton, William (Bishop of Gloucester) 56
Welsh language 12, 50.
See British language
Welshpool 2
Whitaker, John (historian) 38, 40
Whitford, Flintshire 31
Wicklow Hills, Ireland 21
Wilson, Richard 9
Winstay 37
Wye, River 48
Wynn, Elizabeth 32
Wynn, Ellis 31
Wynn family 29, 30, 33
Wynn, Henry 31
Wynn, Mary 32
Wynn, Maurice 30
Wynn (née Gerard), Sydney 31, 32
Wynn, Roger 31
Wynn, Sir John 30
Wynn, Sir Richard 30
Wynn, Sir Watkin 37
Wynn, Thomas 31
Wynn, William 31

Y

Yorke I, Philip 37

* 9 781910 893234 *